COUNSELLING

SHELAGH BRUMFITT

COUNSELLING

SHELAGH BRUMFITT

WINSLOW PRESS
Telford Road, Bicester, Oxon OX6 0TS Tel: Bicester (0869) 244644

Since coming to Sheffield I have been fortunate to find many friends who have given me the support and encouragement to experiment with new ideas and projects. This book is dedicated to them.

First published in 1986 by
Winslow Press, Telford Road, Bicester, Oxon OX6 0TS
Reprinted 1987

ISBN 0 86388 035 5

WP154/Printed by Antony Rowe Ltd, Wiltshire

——————————————— Editor's note ———————————————
The word 'therapist' has been used frequently throughout this text and is intended to include speech therapists, occupational therapists, physiotherapists, nurses and all those in the caring professions.

Contents

CHAPTER 4

COUNSELLING TECHNIQUES / 31

CHAPTER 5

EXERCISES TO DEVELOP COUNSELLING SKILLS / 44

CHAPTER 6

CLINICAL SITUATIONS / 52

CONCLUSION / 64

General Introduction

All of us who work in the caring professions have gained some insights into the implications of disablement and many of us will have shared some of the private distress of patients who have to build or rebuild their lives around a major dysfunction. Indeed, we encounter some cruel ironies: the keen athlete who becomes paraplegic; the artist who loses his sight; the solicitor who becomes alexic. Whether they experience a loss of function caused by an accident or illness, or a dysfunction due to congenital causes, all disabled people share some awareness of what they have lost from the quality of their lives. Have we, as therapists, not often wondered how we would cope with some of the predicaments faced by our patients and their families?

It is the very fact that we do wonder that enables us to be helpful to our patients. Recognizing the possibility that we might ourselves face the same situation can help us to develop a realistic response to a patient's difficulties. It is unlikely that therapists will have suffered the loss of function that they are used to seeing in patients; however, all therapists will have experienced loss of some kind. This could have been the loss of a close family member or a good friend, or the loss of a job, perhaps. The business of getting on with life *without* that important person or thing will be recalled as painful and difficult.

Remembering our own experiences of loss and pain

is a good starting point for counselling. For if we have that awareness of how difficult life can sometimes prove, we can be receptive to our patients' problems and hope to understand them better. Recognizing how someone feels is fundamental to counselling.

To move on from this, exploring how a patient understands him or herself and helping him achieve greater self knowledge and self acceptance, requires warmth and intuition on the part of the therapist . It also requires skill.

This book is intended to offer some new insights and to provide guidelines for increasing personal skill in counselling. Such skill will blend with, and enhance, the therapist's already well-established understanding of the human condition.

Chapter 1
AN INTRODUCTION TO COUNSELLING

WHAT IS COUNSELLING?

Many people understand counselling to be about the offering of advice so that the individual is given some firm direction. However, counselling as a professional activity is a process which moves markedly away from directing the patient, and much more towards encouraging the individual to direct himself. Specific techniques are employed to help people understand themselves better and move forwards more effectively in their lives.

Counselling most often takes place in privacy between two individuals, so that confidentiality and a sense of security are preserved. Although this book addresses itself to speech therapists, physiotherapists, occupational therapists and nurses, the counselling interaction can be applied to many situations such as management skills, the teacher/pupil relationship and other professional areas where there is close contact between people.

A counsellor must be able to respond in a way that allows the distressed patient to develop himself as freely and as helpfully as possible, along his own personal route and not along a road that the counsellor has planned for him. By doing this, the patient is more likely to develop feelings of self-worth and effectiveness. Many distressed people feel that they are trapped in their predicament and that there are no alternative means of perceiving their situation. They feel there are no choices. Thus, for the patient to 'plan his own route' is a major step in his life. He no longer feels that he is doing something because he is compelled to; rather that he is doing something because it seems the most appropriate to him.

The therapist who acts as counsellor will be able to assist in this by employing a variety of techniques. However, what cannot be overestimated is the value of the natural, intuitive response of one human being to another. Some people find that they tend to be sought out by friends who want to discuss a problem. These people obviously have the sort of qualities that make others feel safe enough to confide in them. This intuitive ability to deal with others in distress is something which many therapists already possess and it is a quality which can be used most positively in the counselling interaction.

The ensuing chapters will help therapists and nurses to improve their effectiveness as counsellors by combining their natural responses as carers with some new insights and employing various practical techniques outlined in later chapters.

THE PATIENT OR CLIENT

Before discussing counselling skills in any detail, it is important to consider our notion of what a person is. For example, it is all too easy for the therapist to perceive a patient as, primarily, a mobility disorder or a speech disorder. ("He's a hemiplegic" or "she's a dysphasic".) Clearly, to be effective, the therapist has to attend to the whole person: the human being who is struggling with a loss or disability.

The person occupies a personal framework which allows us to observe him as a separate entity from others. In the same way, the individual has an awareness of his own personal framework which allows him to perceive similarities and differences between himself and others.

Without any understanding of philosophy or

psychology, people seem to have a concept of the self as 'me' and a concept of a self in another person. The familiar phrase, "I'm not feeling myself at the moment", assumes that there is some known and familiar self which is temporarily lost to the speaker. Likewise, "He doesn't seem to be himself today", indicates the speaker's knowledge of the other person and how his behaviour is in some way deviating from his familiar pattern. It is crucial for the developing individual to have a concept of his 'self' as a person. Laing (1969) points out that, in order to live in a sane manner, the individual has to maintain a sense of identity in relation to others. It is impossible to live indefinitely without others; for the sense of identity, of 'self', requires the existence of another by whom one is known.

This recognition of one's own identity, which is considered to be of central importance in psychological well-being, has been further elaborated by Moustakas (1956). He emphasises the importance of acknowledging the individual's own ability to 'know' and organise himself. For professionals working with patients, his emphasis on developing self understanding, rather than relying on external, professional interpretation, has great relevance. Moustakas describes the need for an individual to accept himself because this will allow him to grow and develop his potentialities. The person who cannot accept himself will make much use of his energy defending himself, rather than developing. He emphasizes the need to *grow,* which is present in all of us. Unless we have been emotionally damaged and threatened in some way, we all have an innate capacity to grow towards self fulfillment.

> *"When free from threat the self is more open, that is free to be and to strive for actualisation."*
> *(Moustakas, 1956)*

Notions of what constitutes the 'self' have been discussed for many years by writers such as James (1890), Mead (1934), Rowan (1976) and Bannister and Fransella (1980). What appears to be of central importance is the individual's knowledge of himself and how this compares with his perception of how other people see him. If the individual believes that other people are unaccepting of him because of what he is, then he will not find peace within himself. Therapists frequently meet people who do not feel acceptable to others because of their handicap: such discomfort within the person should not be underestimated. It is essential to take account of these feelings when planning and pursuing treatment with patients.

SOME THEORETICAL APPROACHES TO COUNSELLING

There are many different theoretical perspectives on counselling and much time could be spent describing each approach in detail. However, the main purpose of this book is to introduce the reader to the direct experiences of counselling interaction, and to provide theoretical guidelines.

It is useful, nonetheless, to be aware of the range of approaches that do exist and are in use today. The individual who acts as a counsellor can take up a position with a client that may originate from the rational technique, learning theory, the perceptual-phenomenological approach, or from psychoanalysis or existential psychotherapy. Many counsellors follow one of these approaches quite specifically. Others are more eclectic.

The essential difference in emphasis of these approaches relates to the different underlying understanding of what constitutes the person.

Rational-Emotive theory

Rational-emotive counselling assumes that, although there are strong biological and social forces leading to irrationality, man has the potential for being rational. Albert Ellis (1962) assumes that emotional disturbance and neurosis are irrational thinking and can be overcome by changing that thinking. In consequence, emotions and behaviour need to be made more logical and rational. Ellis's Rational-Emotive therapy aims therefore to help the disturbed individual achieve a new, logical, way of thinking.

Learning theory

According to learning theory the person is someone who operates by means of the pleasure/pain principle. Problems occur when an individual develops a response to an event which might be useful initially, but which later becomes a maladaptive response. For example, the response of nonfluency in speech to a bad reaction from a listener may be the start of a whole range of maladaptive behaviours which form the stuttering syndrome. Anxiety is generally seen to be the driving force behind the response. Wolpe (1958) developed a therapeutic stance called 'reciprocal inhibition' which can be classed as a learning theory approach. Therapy aims to help the individual deal with the anxiety-provoking stimulus in such a way that the pattern of fear and distress in association with the stimulus is broken. This approach is considered to be most useful with people who have specific problems such as phobias, but less useful with people whose distress is caused by environmental factors or more generalised complaints. Learning theory, in the form of behaviour therapy, is frequently used in institutional settings to control behaviours such as addiction or criminality, and where severe behaviour problems accompany subnormality.

The Perceptual-phenomenological field

Perceptual-phenomenological counselling approaches are fairly widely known and used in Great Britain. They are certainly well used in clinical psychology but are also being developed and applied by therapists and social workers. These approaches have in common a major focus on the perceptions of the patient. Client-centred therapy was perhaps the first approach to focus on a concern with the way things appear to the individual. The term 'phenomenological' arises from the philosophical assumption that human knowledge is confined to those things which the individual can directly perceive. The individual generally cannot concern himself with aspects of life which are less directly accessible to him. Client-centred therapy was developed by Carl Rogers during the 1940's. Rogers believes that the client has the answers to most of his own problems, and can find them, given the right sort of space and time. The Rogerian counsellor tries neither to impose change on the client's perception of himself nor to interpret it: he merely reflects it back to the client through his own state of unconditional positive regard (Rogers, 1951).

Rogers believes that the therapeutic relationship that exists in the present can serve as an environment where the client may develop and experiment with new ideas of himself without the problems inherent in his own social context. Once this is achieved the client may transfer some of his experiments to his own social world with a new feeling of personal comfort and self-acceptance.

A second approach — quite different from Rogerian counselling but still perceptually oriented — is Kelly's Personal Construct Theory (1955). Kelly begins from a philosophical position which he calls constructive alternativism. This assumes that every event that has occurred in a person's life, or collectively in the lives of a group of people, is subject to a wide variety of alternative constructions. By a 'construction' he means a discrimination or a distinction. Kelly puts forward the notion that we all see the world in terms of the way we make distinctions: that is by means of our 'constructs'. Each construct discriminates between two poles. A person may construe a food, for example, as either "good for you" or "not good for you".

Kelly sees the individual as a scientist who exists within his own personal system of constructs and who lives his life actively construing future events according to the way in which his individual construct system currently works. Thus, Kelly emphasises the notion of the predictive nature of people. We predict what will happen by our past experience. For example, the way you currently construe the reading of textbooks will allow you to predict how you will find the reading of this particular text.

In terms of therapy, the therapist has to be able to help the patient reconstrue himself and events in order to ease the discomfort of the person in distress. For example, the distressed patient who feels she is worthless and bad, because her husband has left her and wants a divorce, may be able to feel much more positive if she can come to construe her situation as a new challenge, a positive event in her life which may allow her to develop new aspects of herself.

Kelly's approach to therapy is systematic; the person's own construction of his situation is the prime factor in the relationship. The therapist actively encourages a patient to experiment with new ideas, so that opportunities for reconstrual can arise; meanwhile the patient must receive support from the therapist to feel safe enough to experiment.

Gestalt therapy (Perls 1972) is also phenomenological in its orientation. According to Gestalt therapy the person creates his own subjective, and effectively real, world according to his interests and his needs. As for Client-centred therapy, for Gestalt therapists the well-functioning individual is someone who is open to all his experience. Therapy aims to develop the client's awareness towards the goal of the self-actualising person, and to this end Perls believes that a person needs to be in touch with his current, immediate, organismic needs.

The technique of Gestalt therapy differs from other approaches in that little attention is paid to the personal relationship between therapist and patient. In fact, therapy most often takes place in groups where little attention is paid to the actual group process. The patient is encouraged to express his current feelings; the therapist acts as a catalyst, encouraging him to focus all his attention on himself, letting his "self" identify with (and accept) all its feelings and sensations. The therapy, unlike Personal Construct Therapy, is not highly systematised and there has been little research into its effectiveness. This approach is of value particularly to people who have an intellectual approach to life, who may find it hard to express their feelings and thus may become more and more withdrawn.

Psychoanalysis

Psychoanalysis and the psychoanalytical approach to therapy are the classical methods of dealing with unhappy people. The therapies described above have all evolved either directly from, or else in contradiction to, psychoanalysis. The person is seen by the analyst as someone with a confusing array of neurotic desires that stop him reaching his full potential. It is the aim of psychoanalysis to remove the underlying basis of neurotic behaviour by developing a degree of self-reflection which allows the person to confront his neurosis and reach a point where he feels more in control of his own life. (A distorted view that the lay person may have about psychoanalysis is that it is all about sex. This is not what Freud intended. Where the confusion has arisen is in the attention paid to the individual's unconscious drives.) The individual's behaviour is seen as being critically regulated by repressed unconscious thought which Freud considered was based on infantile, bodily desires. Thus Freud believed that behaviour actually represents a sort of inner conversation between unconscious and conscious thought (Freud 1958). Psychoanalysis tends to focus on making the unconscious conscious in order to help the individual unravel some of his conflicts. The relationship between the therapist and patient is crucial: the way the patient perceives the therapist is used to help him work through his conflicts. Past experience, particularly of childhood, is used to help disentangle the patient's present difficulties.

The Existential approach

Finally, the existential approach is more of a quality that can be applied in therapy, rather than a technique in itself. It focuses on the spontaneous moment of experience and the individual is encouraged to deal with 'the here and now' in the therapeutic relationship. The importance of exploring past experiences is played down. The individual is seen as never being separated from the world that he observes i.e. he exists entirely in the world. Existentialists believe that the individual lives in three worlds simultanously — the biological world, without self awareness; the world of interrelationships with other persons, involving mutual awareness; and the world of self identity. The aim of the therapist is to provide a meaningful relationship as a mutual experience to emphasize the patient's 'being in the world' (Kovel 1976). R D Laing, considered to be one of the most notable existential psychotherapists, developed his theories of anti-psychiatry in communities to allow people to enter deeply into their feelings of madness and emerge at the end of the madness with a new-found creative freedom.

In summary, it is important to acknowledge the significance of the therapist's understanding of the person. Clearly, each theory described above starts from a conception of how the individual exists in the world. What we as individuals are is a complex and fascinating question which we may need to rethink and re-evaluate many times as we develop our skills as counsellors. Indeed, the opportunity for such exploration may be of great value, providing its own rewards. In the midst of the anxieties and confusions encountered whilst dealing with patients, increased self-awareness and a deeper understanding of the human condition can only enrich the professional and assist in therapeutic interaction.

Chapter 2
POTENTIAL PROBLEMS IN COUNSELLING

The role of counsellor is one in which some therapists feel ill at ease, doubtless sensing that they are inadequately prepared. This may be because the last decade has seen our professions concentrating on many technological developments, thus temporarily overshadowing the counselling role. It is quite common for a therapist to feel discomfort when faced with a patient in profound emotional distress. The reasons for this appear to be threefold.

Firstly, the traditional medical approach to patients has focussed on the 'disease' rather than on the person who is suffering. The therapy professions have, to a lesser degree, unwittingly absorbed this into their own development. Secondly, the professional boundaries between psychiatry, psychology and the therapies have tended, in all but a few instances, to be rigid; and therapists have not felt free to explore areas in other disciplines. And thirdly, the personal reactions of individual therapists may affect how they handle distress or other strong emotions in their patients.

These three facets of the dilemma will be discussed in the following pages.

THE RELEVANCE OF THE MEDICAL MODEL

The notion of the medical model has developed from the doctors' approach to dealing with disease. A doctor is expected to treat the disease in the patient and thus provide the cure. Unfortunately, this emphasis on disease has meant that the patient's own feelings have been afforded insufficient attention. Some speech therapists will have had experience of members of the medical profession referring to "an interesting laryngeal palsy", almost as if the person who suffered this did not exist. Physiotherapists and occupational therapists can doubtless cite similar examples.

The pathology and symptoms of the complaint are of great significance in themselves; however, there is a danger that too much emphasis may be placed upon the disease or disability and too little on the needs of the whole person.

"People are not mindless bodies; nor are they bodyless minds".
(Clarke, 1975)

In order to be clinically sensitive, therapists must beware of reverting to the traditional approach described above and aim to focus adequate attention on their patients' reactions to problems as well as on the problems themselves.

PROFESSIONAL BOUNDARIES

It is often very difficult for us to know when, or if, to refer a patient to a psychiatrist. Although it is easy enough to see if a patient is seriously deluded, this situation is fairly rare in a therapy context. It does become much more difficult if a therapist is faced with a patient whose mood appears very inconsistent, who says things that are either strange or unduly self-denigrating, or who appears to have serious problems in forming satisfactory human relationships. The therapist only sees the patient for a relatively small amount of time and may either be misled into believing the patient needs psychiatric help because of unusual behaviour in the clinic or, conversely, be misled into believing that the patient is stable because the real situation is withheld from the clinical situation, the clinical environment tending to be slightly artificial.

To the inexperienced therapist, the expression of intense distress during a treatment session, or admission of thoughts of suicide, may seem to indicate a need for immediate referral to .a psychiatrist. However, the vast majority of patients have no need of such measures. For some, breaking down in tears and expressing feelings of hopelessness during a therapy session may be the most useful thing that has happened for weeks. Such an experience, sensitively handled, can be cathartic and positive. However, there are no easy and straightforward answers to these questions.

The stroke patient who expresses a desire to kill himself may not require acute psychiatric care but may need a psychiatric back-up service. The confession may have been one way to communicate to the therapist the intensity of his feelings of despair, following the stroke. Possibly, to have someone acknowledge his distress and allow him to express it may be what is really required. The professional should, if uncertain as to what action is appropriate, discuss the case with an experienced colleague.

It is important to be aware of the fact that, on making a decision to refer a patient to a psychiatrist, the therapist may face problems inherent in that decision. Making such a referral may involve the therapist in irreversible changes in the relationship which he has built up with the patient. If he has previously felt able to express his distress to the therapist because of the quality of that relationship, a perceived change in the therapist's attitude could be inhibiting. Also, the patient may view his therapist's decision to refer to a psychiatrist as a personal rejection ("I cannot take your behaviour, so I am passing you on to somebody else"). If viewed in this way, a referral would not be a useful or positive experience.

There are cases where there is little doubt that a therapist should refer on to a psychiatrist, such as instances of severe and increasing withdrawal or evidence of delusional symptoms, or where there is a previous history of psychiatric problems. But it is important to acknowledge that therapists can often deal very effectively with their patients' emotional conflicts without referring further.

Currently, some psychiatrists encourage therapists to look after their own patients but to 'use' the psychiatrist as a listening ear for discussion of specific difficulties. This is a welcome development and it is to be hoped that it will become increasingly common.

PERSONAL CONFLICT

The work of all therapists has many facets, requiring competence in assessment and remediation, and involving the equally important roles of valued advisor, confidante and counsellor. (Skills in public relations can be a great advantage, too.)

In the clinical environment, where time is often limited, it is not always easy to find the perfect balance between these diverse roles. As assessment and treatment become ever more technical, and as the need for cost-effectiveness apparently increases, there is a slight danger that the rapport between therapist and patient may be undervalued.

It is natural that, in the course of the personal, and often long-term, care given by therapists, a close relationship is developed with patients. One of the problems in each treatment session, however, is to judge how much time should be allotted to encouraging the patient to talk about problems, when this may have to compete with a pressing need for treatment or an assessment that requires completion. Frequently, therapists are inclined to feel guilty if they just allow the patient to talk. If they can resolve this problem from within, then neither party need feel that time is being wasted.

The difficulty experienced by some therapists in

this role may stem from their own attitude to distress. If they construe breaking down, expressing grief and verbalising anxieties as bad, then they are unlikely to feel comfortable about encouraging such behaviour in patients. Only if there is a belief that the open expression of emotion can be a positive and valuable experience, will professionals feel confident to encourage patients to unburden themselves in this way.

Rogers, in an essay about his own personal and professional development, describes peoples' fears about being self-revealing and emotional; and notes how those feelings which are normally considered so unique and private are actually the feelings which unite human beings:

> "I have almost invariably found that the very feeling which has seemed to me most private, most personal, and hence most incomprehensible by others, has turned out to be an expression for which there is a resonance in many other people".
> **(Rogers, 1961)**

GETTING SUPPORT FOR YOURSELF

Traditionally, therapists have tended to follow a medical pattern in treatment, each therapist assuming sole responsibility for his or her own patients. This approach has led to a reluctance among many therapists to ask for advice or to discuss the management of cases and to admit to uncertainties without feeling inadequate or vulnerable.

Recently, psychiatrists, psychologists and social workers have been more open to the notion of support groups for professionals. In a group setting, difficult cases can be discussed, and workers can express their own feelings of frustration, bewilderment or failure. The group members' different perspectives on the situation can allow the individual to explore other ways of helping the patient. If this is done in an accepting, non-competitive atmosphere, members of the group can benefit greatly from the experience.

Another type of professional support involves a more experienced therapist acting as supervisor to another. The supervisor may be another member of the same profession, but might equally be a helpful and interested psychiatrist or psychologist. Again, the therapist can use the time to discuss individual cases but also to explore some of his or her own constructs about people.

It is important to recognise the potential value of a system of professional support. Therapists, who often work intensively with patients, can benefit greatly from opportunities to voice their confusion and to ask questions within such a positive and constructive framework.

RECOGNISING YOUR OWN FEELINGS AND THE IMPORTANCE OF THIS IN THERAPY

However experienced, there will always be situations in therapy which affect the therapist's personal feelings. It is hard not to feel moved by some of our patients' predicaments. What is particularly important, however, is the need to recognise these feelings and work out when they are actually hindering therapy. There are several examples of this.

Sometimes people that we meet as clients may, perhaps in physical features or personality, remind us of someone we knew in the past. If the reminder is about a person who we disliked or feared in some way, then the patient in question may prove more than usually difficult to deal with. Provided the therapist can recognise these negative feelings, it is likely that they can be put to one side and that treatment can continue. However, if the professional's feelings are not recognised or managed effectively then treatment with that patient may well be unsuccessful.

Situations that patients are in, or problems that they bring to the clinic, may also give rise to uncomfortable personal feelings. The distressed spouse of a stroke patient may remind the professional of a mother or father. It is not uncommon for a therapist to identify too closely with a situation of this kind, and consequently to deal less effectively with the problems.

Just as certain patients may stimulate negative emotions in therapists, others may actually be found disconcertingly attractive. Whatever the professional relationship (be it between solicitor and client, shopkeeper and customer or doctor and patient), and however briskly transactions may be handled, there is no escaping the fact that some members of the opposite sex will appear very attractive, professionally unwelcome though this may be. If the attraction is so great as to interfere with the effectiveness of the treatment being offered, then the professional may be well advised to find someone to talk to about this. It could be that to transfer the patient to another therapist would be the simplest solution.

COUNSELLING THAT APPEARS TO BE A FAILURE

Although it may be easy for a therapist to see that a patient needs counselling, the patient may not be as able or as willing to acknowledge it himself. This may cause the therapist a sense of 'hitting one's head against a brick wall' when trying to help the patient explore some of the things that are troubling him. Some patients may be extremely resistant to a counselling approach, and feel very threatened at the prospect of exposing any psychological wounds. Others, whilst able to articulate the nature of their problems to the therapist, may find it more difficult to move on from that position or to view their difficulties in any alternative way.

One of the conflicts for a therapist is in worrying whether a patient may be failing to respond because of inadequate professional technique or primarily because of the way that particular patient 'is'. In situations such as these, the therapist would be well advised to talk through the case with a supportive colleague.

There will be occasions when the therapist can perceive problems in a patient but can equally appreciate that the patient is really not psychologically ready to deal with them. It is important to be able to acknowledge this to oneself and to feel comfortable with the decision to defer deeper exploration and, for the time being at least, to let the patient 'be'.

Sometimes a patient may find he has talked about feelings so difficult for him to deal with that he does not wish to pursue them any further with the therapist: very occasionally a patient may decide to terminate therapy because of this. The professional may feel understandably uncomfortable, wondering if the situation has been mishandled. With hindsight, he may regret that discussions with the patient evolved as they did; or the conclusion may have to be drawn that this individual found his therapist's attempts to help him too threatening to handle at that time.

These dilemmas do occur (see Chapter VI, example 4) and all that can be done is to review the situation as objectively as possible, to learn from any obvious mistakes made, and to endeavour not to be too hard on oneself as a therapist. Sometimes, too, the patient knows what is best for him, and we as therapists have to accept that.

ANSWERING PATIENTS' QUESTIONS

Because of the nature of counselling, which aims to develop the person's skill in dealing with his own life, it may be difficult to know how to respond to the patient who asks directly for an opinion.

However, sometimes a patient asks a question without particularly wanting an answer. The question may simply be a signal to the therapist that discussion of a certain topic would be welcome. For example, if a disability is making it difficult for someone to function at work as well as before, the therapist may be asked the question, "Do you think I should give up my job?" The most useful response to this sort of question is to understand that the patient may not in fact be asking for an answer but for a chance to talk through his feelings about the whole situation.

CONCLUSION

It may seem disheartening to confront a range of potential problems in counselling before exploring the techniques. The intention is not to discourage but to acknowledge openly some of the issues that are difficult for therapists to deal with. These are quite likely to be concerns that some readers have already considered for themselves.

Chapter 3
IMPORTANT ISSUES FOR THE THERAPIST TO CONSIDER WHEN COUNSELLING

RECOGNISING EMOTIONAL AGES

Readers will be familiar with the differences between chronological and mental ages. A more abstract concept is that of emotional age. Most of us have fairly stereotyped notions of how people of certain ages should behave, and we may have subjective impressions of individuals being either immature or mature for their age.

Whilst it is not possible to specify what behaviour and emotional responses can be expected from different age groups, it is important to be aware that not all 'adult' people cope with difficult circumstances in an emotionally 'adult' way.

For example, the wife of a stroke patient may not react to her husband's difficulties with sympathy and understanding but, instead, perceive his handicaps in terms of the impact they have had on her. Indeed, she may respond to the limitations imposed on her in the same way as she responded to being limited as a child, expressing both anger and resentment. In a situation such as this, it is helpful if emotional immaturity is identified by the professionals involved. When attempting to help this woman, allowances should be made, for her reaction to stress may have changed little in adult life, and emotional maturation cannot be hurried.

THE EFFECT OF PAST EXPERIENCES

Whether we are consciously aware of it or not, we are all affected by our past experiences. Sometimes, events in our present lives may trigger off memories from the past and our feelings may be heightened in consequence. This applies equally to patients who could be attempting to cope with this kind of emotional reaction, whilst at the same time being required to concentrate on a demanding therapy programme. It may be sufficient for the therapist simply to be aware of this; but it is very likely that the patient would be pleased to talk about what is on his mind.

For example, a woman attending an Out-patient clinic and feeling unnerved when required to walk through the hospital to reach the appropriate department, may be reliving the painful emotions associated with the death of a close relative in that same hospital years ago. This reaction, though quite unrelated to present circumstances, is nonetheless a problem to the individual concerned, and may affect her progress. Equally, a patient who is required to do exercises in reading or writing as a part of his therapy for aphasia, could respond negatively because they remind him of some uncomfortable learning experiences in childhood.

Skenderian (1983) describes the case of a man who suffered a CVA and was subsequently paralysed, with additional speech impairment. This man had been a prisoner-of-war in a concentration camp and had suffered long and deeply from the indignities and restrictions. The experiences of the CVA brought back many of the feelings he had had about the concentration camp and he was forced to relive some of the psychological agonies. Treatment was slowed up by this and it was vital to acknowledge the significance of this man's feelings. Until he was able to acknowledge some of these with a therapist, his progress in the rehabilitation programme was minimal.

Even in less unusual circumstances, adults with acquired disability may feel intensely distressed by their handicaps. It is helpful to explore with them their past experiences of disablement or loss, for childhood injuries or anxieties may be among the causes of such a reaction.

LOSS AND GRIEF

The therapist will be in contact with a great many people who have experienced some form of bereavement, either by literally losing a spouse through death, or by physical loss which relates to a specific illness — such as loss of mobility and speech following a stroke or head injury.

Speck (1978) discusses the problems faced by people who lose a part of themselves because of surgery or some medical problem (eg. amputation of a limb, miscarriage or loss of sight). In most areas of medicine, patients may experience the psychological effects of major loss. Obstetric and gynaecological problems such as stillbirth or hysterectomy are pertinent examples. The woman who gives birth to a handicapped child experiences a profound sense of loss as she grieves for the normal child she had anticipated. One of the difficulties in dealing with loss in this context is that the mother has to care for the abnormal child at the same time as grieving for the idealised infant that is 'lost'. Corney (1981) describes the frequent, immediate response as one of disbelief and denial (typical of most bereavement reactions), but also offers very clear examples of this in the parent's tendency to seek an alternative, less negative diagnosis or a more positive prognosis from medical staff.

The reaction of a person to amputation can be seen, too, as grieving for what has been lost (Murray Parkes, 1975, Dembo, 1952). Murray Parkes notes that, for amputees, one of the difficulties in coping with the loss is the fact that they are constantly reminded of the amputated limb as they go about their daily lives. They are forced to take account of the fact that they are no longer functioning with four flexible limbs. A parallel may be drawn here with people who have acquired communication problems (eg. aphasics or laryngectomy patients) who experience constant reminders of their difficulty in speaking.

Some suggestions as to the varying degrees of impact of a loss have been put forward. Safilios-Rothschild (1970) suggests that the easier it is for an individual to hide his disability, the more difficulty he will have in incorporating it into his self image. Shibutani (1961) and Strauss (1962) feel it is more closely related to the core self-concept. If the affected part of the body is central to the self-concept (eg. the breast as symbolising sexuality in women), then the physical 'disability' (ie. mastectomy) may be extremely hard for the patient to accept. Thus, grieving may prove difficult or be psychologically blocked in some way.

Certainly, in many of the patients seen by members of the therapy professions, the dysfunction relates to a 'hidden' loss such as dyslexia, or agnosia. However, it may also relate to those losses where the body image has been distorted, as in hemiplegia or progressive disease.

SPECIFIC REACTIONS TO LOSS

The way that people react to loss has been examined by many authors including Freud (1917), Hinton (1967), Bowlby (1980) and Murray Parkes (1975). Certainly, a person's response to a major bereavement will not be one of straightforward sorrow. What does seem to be the case is that such a loss gives rise to a turmoil of emotions which take a long time to be worked through. This process of grieving has been helpfully defined by Murray Parkes (1975) and Bowlby (1980). Both descriptions have been based on observations of people who have lost a significant person, but they can be usefully applied to individuals who have suffered any sort of major loss.

Bowlby (1980) describes four phases of mourning

through which individuals may move after losing a significant person. He points out that these phases are not clear-cut and an individual may oscillate between two at a time; however, an overall sequence can be discerned. The four phases he describes are:

"1. Phase of numbing that usually lasts from a few hours to a week, and may be interrupted by outbursts of extremely intense distress and/or anger.

2. Phase of yearning and searching for the lost figure, lasting some months and sometimes for years.

3. Phase of disorganisation and despair.

4. Phase of a greater or lesser degree of reorganisation."

Murray Parkes (1975) had previously defined seven typical features of bereavement:

"1. A process of realisation, ie the way in which the bereaved moves from denial or avoidance of recognition towards acceptance of the loss.

2. An alarm reaction — anxiety, restlessness and the physiological accompaniments of fear.

3. An urge to search for and to find the lost person in some form.

4. Anger and guilt, including outbursts directed against those who press the bereaved person towards premature acceptance of his loss.

5. Feelings of internal loss of self, or mutilation.

6. Identification phenomena — the adoption of traits, mannerisms or symptoms of the lost person, with or without a sense of his presence within the self.

7. Pathological variants of grief, ie. the reaction may be excessive and prolonged, or inhibited and inclined to emerge in a distorted form."

Of particular importance for therapists is Murray Parkes' feature relating to the process of realisation.

Frequently, therapists have to begin some form of remediation with a patient who has not fully understood what has been lost, either because the reality is too overwhelming to be faced, or because the patient has not yet been able to see the long-term implications of the loss. He will be feeling insecure and bewildered and will be more likely to respond to the therapist if he is treated with sensitivity and understanding.

Also of importance is the patient's searching for the 'lost person' (Bowlby and Murray Parkes). Although there is no real 'lost person' in this context, patients do mourn the loss of the person that they were before they were ill. They can also be preoccupied by thoughts of the person that they might have been.

Readers have perhaps had some experience of patients getting angry with them. As Murray Parkes observes, this is not unusual in a patient who is grieving, especially if the therapist is making him more aware of his limitations when carrying out an assessment of his difficulties. The alarm reaction can be seen to accompany anger, great anxiety becoming evident as the disabled person comes to understand more fully what he has lost. When carrying out assessments, professionals must be acutely conscious of the emotional responses of their patients.

Murray Parkes' recognition of pathological variants of grief is also of relevance for therapists, for some patients find it hard to let themselves 'feel' their distress. Many months or even years after the event has occurred, some are seen to react intensely to reminders of their loss, thereby revealing that they have been suppressing their feelings and did not satisfactorily 'work through' the normal process of grieving.

HELPING THE PATIENT TO DEAL WITH LOSS

The person with an acquired problem in movement or communication needs to have that loss acknowledged in a way that shows the extent and depth of their loss has been fully understood. Because physiotherapists, occupational therapists and speech therapists meet such a vast range of problems (some of them very severe), it may be hard to appreciate that the sense of loss experienced, for example, by someone with relatively mild difficulties, can be as acute as that of a person who is hemiplegic and globally aphasic. What is significant is not the degree of handicap but the way in which the problem affects the patient's self-image and central concept of himself. Whether grossly or mildly impaired, there is a painful awareness that he is no longer the person he was.

It is undoubtedly very reassuring to a patient to have his feelings acknowledged and to be told that his emotional responses are a normal part of the grieving process. Time should be allowed for him to talk about exactly how he is feeling and to identify what has and has not changed. Deciding exactly what has changed could take a period of some months, as the implications of lost communication or physical skills may only become apparent as each old and familiar situation is retested by the impaired patient. There may, therefore, be recurrences of distress and sadness at different stages, when the patient faces new situations and feels defeated.

Entangled with this grief over what has been lost is the person's confusion over who he has now become. ("If I am no longer who I was, then who am I now?") In small, gradual steps, the patient will need support as he gains new insights about himself. These may be painful insights: for example, if the speech therapist exposes to the aphasic how far-reaching are his limitations in verbal expression. If an attempt is made to accelerate his rate of acceptance of these difficulties he may respond with anger and denial.

Efforts can be focused on helping the patient feel positive about gaining increased control over his movement or his speech, but the professional must be alert to what is happening in the treatment session. Outbursts of anger may be directed at him or her because of what the patient perceives to be attempts at 'teasing out' his weakness.

Gradually, as treatment continues, each patient attempts to build a new identity. Certainly this new identity may feel totally unacceptable to him, but at least it is some structure from which to reconstrue his life. As stated by Murray Parkes (1975), the patient may need to resort to a regular searching for the 'lost self' as a way of reassuring himself of what he used to be. This often takes the form of talking about pre-morbid events and achievements, and the need should be met with a positive response.

Over a period of months, an acceptable new identity is sought. For many with acquired disabilities, there will never be a complete return to how they were before. During the rehabilitation programme, sufficient 'emotional time' must be allowed for the individual to gain a degree of acceptance of the status quo. This will vary greatly from person to person, but in a few cases the anguish, anger and non-acceptance of loss persist for years. In such circumstances, where grief is fixed and unresolved, a therapist may consider seeking suggestions from a colleague in the psychiatric service. Alternatively, direct referral to a psychiatrist may be thought most appropriate.

HELPING THE SPOUSE COME TO TERMS WITH THE NEW CIRCUMSTANCES

In cases of acquired disability, whatever the impact on the patient, there is no doubt that the change in his circumstances will have had a profound effect on those closest to him. Most frequently, the greatest strain is felt by the spouse. Reactions characteristically resemble those of bereavement, as previously described, for they too have experienced loss. They grieve for a familiar and loved person who was once so active but who is now, at best, sad and bewildered, and at worst, unresponsive.

Here, the therapist can help by allowing the spouse time to talk about his or her reaction to the situation. Feelings of anger are not uncommon: anger that they have been let down in some way; anger that the spouse is left to deal with everything. There may also be a strong sense of guilt. ("Why am I having these selfish thoughts?"; "I shouldn't be angry with my hemiplegic husband"; "He can't help it really"). These feelings may be further complicated by previously unresolved conflicts within the partnership. Time must be made available for a spouse to express these feelings without a sense of guilt. Reassurance can be offered to a wife, for example, that she is entitled to experience negative reactions, and that her mixed emotions are neither unnatural nor unique.

If a spouse finds these negative feelings frightening or disturbing, he or she may react by denying the degree of loss and failing to face the reality of the situation. Where this occurs, counselling is necessary but may be difficult and delicate.

Problems may also arise in marriages where partners have to take on unaccustomed roles. For example, the wife who has been used to having her husband deal with the financial aspects of their life may now find that, because of his stroke, she has to assume that responsibility. The problem is not just a practical issue, though learning all about the family finances at a late stage in life is no easy task. More disturbing is the realisation that the way she previously defined herself — 'knew herself' — is no longer relevant. Role-reversal of this kind puts a great strain on many couples.

One problem a therapist may face is the difficulty that arises when both patient and spouse want to use the therapist as counsellor. Certainly, the therapist will feel divided loyalties; and it is possible the patient may feel betrayed in some way if his therapist appears to be supporting his wife. The therapist can offer a degree of insightful support, which may in many cases be all that is necessary to help the well partner through the rehabilitation period. However, if there are conflicts between the partners which relate to previously unre-solved difficulties, then the therapist might be wise to guide the spouse towards other contacts for support. This is not intended to imply that the therapist lacks the skill to deal with the spouse's difficulty. However, it does acknowledge the fact that, whilst counselling and remediation of a patient are integral parts of therapy, long-term marital or family counselling cannot be given priority in this context.

Chapter 4
COUNSELLING TECHNIQUES

INTRODUCTION

There is a tendency to feel that counselling skills are impossible to learn, because no one is able to provide the novice with a script. Often counsellors in training complain that they "still don't know what they are supposed to say".

It is important to understand that no script can be provided. The developing counsellor must aim to acquire a set of skills which can be sensitively applied within a counselling session. Every counselling relationship has its own unique qualities and the counsellor has to respond with relevance to each.

The techniques outlined in this chapter can be described as non-directive methods of counselling. A fundamentally different approach, namely directive counselling, involves the giving of technical advice and advising a patient what action to take. Directive methods are also used in social skills training and anxiety management techniques.

Non-directive counselling focuses on the individual's self growth, encourages the person to make his or her own choices and to take responsibility for them. Counselling approaches of the perceptual-phenomenological type are most relevant to those techniques which are designed to help the patient work out his own answers to his problems, by exploring his reactions without intruding on his perception of self. Readers are referred to pages 9 to 11 for further discussion of the approaches of Rogers and Kelly whose work has had a major influence on the philosophy of this book.

The therapist may be alerted to a patient's need for counselling by overt signs of distress; however, it is more common for some passing remark to signal that there are issues causing concern. People give expression to their frustrations and anxieties in a variety of ways, and the professional must be sensitive to these coded messages.

There are two main reasons why patients may find it hard to talk about their problems:

(a) They may have difficulty recognizing exactly what their feelings are about their predicament: they 'feel', yet they cannot put a label to it.

(b) They may not feel sufficiently secure to expose their anxieties to the therapist, making it difficult for the professional to be of help.

The approaches described below are intended to help the therapist gain a deeper insight into the patient's difficulties by exploring with him some aspects of his disability. As they look together at his circumstances and consider his reactions, a relationship of trust can be established over a period of time. When the patient has developed a fuller understanding of his situation and feels secure in their relationship, he is better able to make significant changes.

ATTENDING TO THE PERSON ('NON VERBAL LISTENING')

The most traditional form of psychoanalysis allows the therapist to listen without offering many verbal interventions. Although this 'silent listening' can be disconcerting for inexperienced counsellors, it is a valuable approach. Members of the caring professions will be familiar with using their own speech as a stimulus or to give instructions in treatment. Listening silently is a more difficult skill to acquire, for the patient needs to feel safe to talk at length about a problem and yet feel confident that he is being given the listener's full attention.

Three ways of giving attention without actually speaking are given below:

(a) providing good eye contact

(b) responding by facial expression to what is being said

(c) sitting in a position that does not threaten the patient yet allows the therapist to show interest. This involves making sure that you are not sitting on opposite sides of a desk, but are sitting at an angle which allows eye contact but avoids causing embarrassment or discomfort.

LISTENING SKILLS

It is difficult to analyse the attributes of a good listener. Whilst some people appear to shy away from those with problems to discuss, others have qualities which make them easy to confide in. Many of the following features may be identified in such a person:

Features of a good listener:

(a) does not interrupt.

(b) does not appear to be judgemental about the person's problem.

(c) is accepting of what the person says.

(d) does not undervalue the person's problem by describing an event of worse proportions.

(e) makes it clear that there is time for the person to talk.

(f) avoids the direct giving of advice.

(g) attempts to clarify what is obscure.

(h) gives the speaker full attention.

APPROPRIATE INTERJECTIONS

It is not advocated that a counsellor should remain silent throughout a session; indeed, speech can be used sparingly to great advantage. For example, it is helpful to indicate that the patient has been heard and understood; and questions may be asked in order to clarify what has been said. The aim is to interject in ways which will help the speaker to 'move on', perhaps developing a different perspective on his problem, or beginning to construe his situation in a more positive way.

SHOWING YOU HAVE UNDERSTOOD

A person who is finding it hard to make sense of his troubles, may struggle to articulate his feelings to others, lacking confidence in his ability to convey what he really means. If this is the case, then the counsellor can make a positive contribution just by saying "I understand" or "I can imagine that you feel like that". This kind of simple reassurance may be quite sufficient at that point in the session.

QUESTIONING THE SPEAKER

Naturally, the therapist may not always understand what the speaker is trying to say. In this case, some carefully worded questions may help him to organize his thoughts better, so that the two can perhaps explore the ground in greater depth. However, it must be remembered that questions can be threatening if a person is feeling vulnerable, so a conscious effort should be made to avoid using questions that might sound like interrogation.

There are two types of questions that can be considered in this context:

Closed questions:

These are used in the typical case history format and often require no more than a Yes/No answer. The questions are generally very specific.

eg. Do you find you dribble a lot?
Does he have trouble sleeping?

Open questions:

These are less direct and less specific. They permit the speaker to choose how to respond, and are often used to help a patient get started. With this type of question the counsellor can appear accepting, showing that whatever the patient chooses to say is "right".

eg. How have things been recently?
What sort of difficulties do you have?

EXERCISE A

The reader is invited to rate these questions in order of openness. *(See Appendix, page 68.)*

1. Would you like cream with these strawberries?
2. How do you get on talking to strangers?
3. What sort of things does she say to you?
4. When did you have your stroke?
5. At what age did she sit up?
6. How are you?
7. Shall I fetch you something from the shop?

When wording open questions, it is helpful to indicate to the patient that the counsellor, too, is wondering about something. A tentative "I wonder if . . . ?" or "Does it seem . . . ?" is much less threatening than a direct question.

Reflection

This is a form of verbal response which invites the speaker to pause and consider what he has just said. The counsellor does not attempt to direct or give advice, but just reflects back to the speaker what he has said.
eg. Patient:

"Oh, I suppose it was all right at that school. It was er . . .

different from what I was used to. Em. I suppose it was rather nursery-like."

Therapist:

"Nursery-like?"

Description of the school as 'nursery-like' could imply many different things, and the counsellor chose to reflect this back to the speaker who was then invited to explain further, and think more deeply about what 'nursery-like' really meant to her.

Many people say things without first giving them careful consideration. But, for the troubled person who is trying to understand himself and his circumstances better, opportunities to reflect are most valuable.

The technique of reflection may also serve as a non-intrusive response, sustaining the dialogue between patient and therapist by the convention of turn-taking and yet interrupting the flow as little as possible. Reflection does not stimulate the speaker to digress but encourages the focusing of attention on an issue.

The following are two samples of client/counsellor interaction, the first being an extract from a dialogue between a therapist and a patient with a stammer. They are intended to highlight some of the questioning and listening techniques discussed above:

SAMPLE I

Therapist: *"Well, how have things been during the week?"*

Patient: "Not so good I'm afraid." (offers nothing further)

Therapist: *"What sort of things haven't been good?"*

Patient: "Oh, I don't know. I've just felt a bit fed up. I don't feel I'm getting anywhere. I thought my speech was better, but it's not."

Therapist: *"What happened to make you feel like that?"*

Patient: (Sighs) "Well, I went out with that girl I was telling you about last week and, oh God, it was dreadful. I made a right fool of myself. (Sighs) We went to a pub and I tried to order the drinks in front of her and I 'blocked' like mad."

Therapist: *"Mm."*

Patient: "You know, she hadn't seen me stammer properly before. I think she didn't realise I had any speech difficulty."

Therapist: *"What do you think she felt like?"*

Patient: "What did she feel like? (Pause) Em, well she didn't say anything about it but she went and sat down at a table and waited for me to bring the drinks over."

Therapist: *"What did she do when you brought them over?"*

Patient: "Er, she asked me if I'd got a stammer and so I told her all about it and about the course I've been on and everything."

Therapist: *"And what was she like when you'd told her?"*

Patient: "Oh, she was OK. She told me about her younger brother who hadn't spoken properly until he was four."

Therapist: *"Did that make it more comfortable for you? It sounds to me as if she was trying to show you she understood."*

Patient: "Does it?" (Long pause)
"I suppose it was, but I hadn't thought about it like that. I was just aware all the time about how stupid and bad I was."

Therapist: *"Stupid and bad?"* (Reflection)

Patient: (Grins) "I suppose that sounds a bit over the top now. But I don't know; I just keep feeling I'm no good and a failure because of my speech."

Therapist: *"Do you really believe that you are a failure?"*

Patient: (Long pause) "Deep down I believe I'm OK. It just comes over me every now and then, this feeling of not being any good. It swamps me sometimes."

Therapist: *"Well. What you must try to hang on to is that belief that's deep down, you know. That's the bit you have to use and work on."*

COMMENT

In this extract, some important points are worth

noting: in particular, the detailed exploration by the therapist. When the patient states that he has not had a good week, the therapist questions with the aim of establishing what has caused concern and does not let the patient's statement pass.

Of particular significance is the therapist's emphasis on the girlfriend's behaviour: it is clear the patient was too absorbed by his own feelings to notice the girl's sympathetic reaction and her attempts at making him feel better. Here, the therapist helps the patient find a new construction of the situation, by careful use of open questions and some reflection.

Notice, too, that the therapist helps the patient think seriously about his feelings of failure. No attempt is made to 'jolly him along', and his feelings are acknowledged. However, positive points are drawn to his attention. Note that the therapist does not react to the patient's worries by becoming anxious herself. If that were to happen, he would become very alarmed.

The second transcript is a short extract from a long and complicated conversation between a counsellor and the wife of a young man, seriously injured a year previously in an industrial accident:

SAMPLE II

Wife: "I just wish I could put the clock back to how we were a few years ago. Now we just don't seem to get on very well."

Therapist: *"Don't seem to get on very well?"*

Wife: "Well, it's just that we don't seem to enjoy being together very much."

Therapist: *"What seems to happen when you are together?"*

Wife: "Oh, we get on each other's nerves and he picks on me. He's forever telling me that I don't do things properly — you know, things in the house — cleaning, tidying up."

Therapist: *"What do you feel about that?"*

Wife: "It's damned unfair! Honestly, I work hard, trying

to look after the house and make sure he doesn't do too much. He doesn't know how much he's protected. He thinks because he's managed to get back to work, then he's back to normal. But it's not true: I prop him up all the time!"

Therapist: *"And how does that make you feel?"*

Wife: (Pause) "Em . . . I suppose I feel like he doesn't appreciate what I'm doing; like I'm doing all this and it's wasted. I might as well not bother because he doesn't care really."

Therapist: *"Doesn't care?"*

Wife: "That's right. He doesn't care."

COMMENT

In this extract, the value of certain responses is highlighted. In the initial statement from the wife, there are two potential themes which the therapist could pursue — the past life that the wife and husband had together; and the present difficulties in the relationship. The therapist chooses to reflect back to the wife the area of difficulty in the present. The wife is able to use this reflection to elaborate further, giving the therapist a chance to put their situation in context. However, it is necessary to explore further, by gentle questioning, the nature of the tensions at home. It is achieved, in this instance, by use of a closed question: "What seems to happen when you are together?" The question is concrete and the wife responds by offering her own perceptions of her husband's attitude and behaviour. This is followed by use of two open questions which explore the wife's feelings, giving her the opportunity to relieve herself of some of her resentment. Finally, a second use of reflection produces confirmation of how the lady construes her husband's attitude to her.

FINDING A THEME IN THE PATIENT'S EXPERIENCES

In order to help a patient recognise his own feelings and thereby reach a better understanding of himself, it can be useful to invite him to remember previous events and to consider whether feelings experienced at that time were in any way similar to his present emotions.

For example, it is possible he will be experiencing feelings of frustration and perhaps hopelessness about his condition, though he may not have articulated them. When invited to consider any events in the past when he felt 'the same as he does now', he may describe trying to climb a steep hill when out walking; learning to drive; struggling to decorate a large room when everything was going wrong.

It is useful then to explore what he remembers of his feelings at that time, and how he dealt with them. For example, did he find it was helpful to talk to someone about it at the time, or did he keep it to himself? Such discussions can help the patient to understand better his own reactions to his present difficulties.

Below are some exercises which illustrate the idea of thinking in themes. Readers are invited to consider their own life experiences:

Think about all the occasions:

(a) when you have found something difficult to do.

(b) when you have felt guilty. What had you done on those occasions to make you feel like that?

(c) when you have felt embarrassed.

(d) when you have felt extremely happy and self confident.

Note that it takes some time to summon up and evaluate one's memories. The counsellor should bear this in mind when asking patients to do the same.

THE USE OF TOUCH

Many therapists will already be accustomed to touching their patients during the course of assessment and remedial activity. Therapeutic procedures frequently necessitate some degree of physical contact. Over and above this, it can be observed that distressed people who are experiencing painful emotions do derive some comfort from being touched. There are, of course, exceptions; but for many patients, a friendly arm around the shoulders or the squeezing of a hand, can bring some comfort and reassurance.

Touch may also be used to help a patient compose him or herself in preparation for returning to the business of daily living, having perhaps expressed intense emotions during a counselling session. A comforting touch can aid that transition and reinforces the moral support which has been offered by the professional during the course of their verbal interaction.

MAKING SURE YOU UNDERSTAND WHAT THE PATIENT IS SAYING

Given that the vast majority of people find it extremely hard to put their feelings into words, it is important for a counsellor to ask for clarification if a word or remark (which may have meaning to the speaker) is nonetheless not very clear to the listener. For example, one patient described himself as having an 'adult mind'. Superficially, the therapist may have had notions about what that meant, but to understand precisely what that concept meant to the patient, further exploration was felt necessary.

There is no set technique recommended for examining with a patient his 'understanding' of a word; but the therapist needs to be generally alert to the language that each patient uses. Often, reflecting back what the patient has just said may be sufficient. On other occasions, it may be necessary to ask the patient more directly about what he means, using either open or closed questions as previously described.

SUMMARISING WHAT THE PATIENT HAS SAID

A patient may spend some time telling the counsellor how he feels, volunteering a lot of information in a hurried and disorganised way. Interaction between the speaker and the listener can be assisted if the latter attempts, at intervals, to summarise what has been said. Statements and facts can be offered to the patient, ostensibly to check out whether the therapist has actually understood what he was trying to say. This again gives the patient an opportunity to think about what he has said and to decide whether this summary is in fact accurate. An example is given in the dialogue below:

Patient: "Well, you see, it all happened over the summer holidays. My parents suddenly said they were going to get divorced and that's when it happened. The money was coming from my father and it's run out. My mother is living away now with her sister, and so that's why the money has run out. It's been hell, really. If my father had been able to pay, it would have been all right. But it's my mother, you see."

Therapist: *"So what happened was that, during the summer, your parents decided to divorce and your source of money from your father ran out because he was having to pay for your mother. Is that right?"*

Patient: "Yes, that's it. Now I just have to sort things out from there."

DEALING WITH SEVERE ANGER OR DISTRESS IN A PATIENT

It is sometimes inevitable that a patient will express deep emotions in the clinical setting; and the therapist may find the experience disconcerting, particularly if her patient's anger appears to be potentially dangerous. Although extreme situations such as this are met less often by us than by social workers, psychiatrists or prison officers, it is useful to have considered a hypothetical event and how one might respond.

Above all, the therapist should endeavour to remain calm, resisting any inclination to respond in anger to the patient's anger. Nothing should be said or done which might increase the intensity of his feelings, but the counsellor may work gently towards a situation where the anger can be expressed safely.

If he is severely distressed then, again, the therapist must endeavour to create a stable and secure atmosphere. The trusting relationship with a therapist may be the only context in which an individual feels free to give vent to pent up emotion. When intense grief or frustration are being expressed, acceptance and understanding are essential.

Personality disorders and behaviour difficulties, perhaps resulting from brain damage, may require a modified approach. Discussion with professional colleagues is most valuable in these circumstances.

The patient is likely to find it helpful to talk about an emotional outburst, in retrospect, examining the reasons why he felt so distressed and discussing how he feels about the incident now.

If anger has been directed towards the counsellor, it is also helpful to explore with the patient whether the therapist did or said anything that triggered off the outburst. Open discussion is most important, as is the need to reassure the patient that he is still accepted and that the relationship of trust has not been damaged.

CONCLUSION

Therapists who are accustomed to dealing primarily with assessment and remediation may at first feel ill at ease in the more passive role of counsellor, as described in the preceding pages. An ability to 'wait' and 'listen' may take time and patience to acquire; but having perfected these skills, therapists should feel more confident about allowing the patient time to work things out for himself. If the emotional needs of an individual are acknowledged and handled with sensitivity, then the patient is more likely to make progress in his treatment. Meanwhile, the professional experiences the additional satisfaction of having responded to the 'whole' person, and not simply to his disability.

Chapter 5

EXERCISES TO DEVELOP COUNSELLING SKILLS

Exercises included in this chapter are intended to help increase the reader's awareness. Before attempting to put into practice some of the techniques described in Chapter Four, you are invited to reflect on how you might react to what a patient says; and how easy it might be to construe how the patient is feeling, from remarks he may make in passing during a treatment session. An accurate evaluation makes it much easier to offer positive help.

It is also a great asset to be able to find the right words to say; and opportunities are given here to consider what you *might* have said in certain circumstances. It will be seen that sensitivity and an open mind are valuable attributes for an aspiring counsellor.

EXERCISE B.
INTERPRETING HOW THE PATIENT FEELS

Mark what you consider to be the most relevant descriptions of the feelings of these patients. More than one description may well apply to each. (See Appendix, page 86).

1. **Woman recovering from road accident:** "This time in hospital has been good for me in many ways. I've actually had time to think about my life and what I've been doing for the last few years; and I realise I want to make some changes."

This woman feels: (a) peaceful (b) positive (c) pessimistic (d) alarmed (e) friendly (f) surprised (g) grateful (h) relieved.

2. **Parent of mentally handicapped adult:** "She's been a gift to us in many ways. She is so trusting and loving that you can't help but love her back in the same way. But the worry now is about the future. Her father died two years ago and here I am not getting any younger. What will happen to her? She can't manage by herself. I just can't stop worrying about it."

This person feels: (a) unaware (b) angry (c) distressed (d) realistic (e) self centred (f) hysterical (g) bitter (h) amused (i) self confident (j) preoccupied.

3. **Geriatric patient:** "She was ever such a good girl to us. I do miss her. I know you can't stop your children going their own way but I do wish they hadn't gone as far away as Canada. I'll never see my grandchildren again."

This person feels: (a) distressed (b) empty (c) enthusiastic (d) cocky (e) frightened (f) grief-stricken (g) hopeless (h) awed (i) angry (j) friendly.

4. **Transexual male who wants to change to a female:** "Sometimes I lie on my bed and dream about the future. In a few years time, I'll be able to find a man of my own and maybe we'll be able to live together. I know I'm going to be much better as a woman. I feel much better with make-up on and nice clothes."

This person feels: (a) alarmed (b) unrealistic (c) anxious (d) optimistic (e) pessimistic (f) self confident (g) irresponsible (h) overwhelmed (i) fed up (j) idealistic.

5. **Wife of man who suffered a CVA three months ago:** "It's been difficult since he came home. I don't know what's the matter with him. In hospital he was all right; seemed to know what I was saying. But now! Oh dear, he just carries on and doesn't take any notice of what I say at all."

This person feels: (a) happy (b) bewildered (c) incompetent (d) lost (e) angry (f) enthusiastic (g) tired (h) lively (i) anxious (j) hostile.

6. **Adult physically handicapped man:** "I can't tell you how sick I am of everybody's patronising attitude; their boring, sickly sympathy. What the Hell do people know about what I feel like? They've no idea at all."

This person feels: (a) optimistic (b) confused (c) angry (d) misunderstood (e) amused (f) indignant (g) cynical (h) isolated.

7. **Child with specific learning difficulties:** "I know Mummy and Daddy are upset about me. Sometimes they make me upset because I know they want me to be as good as everybody else at school. I wish I found it all easy. I get really fed up with having to do extra homework."

This child feels: (a) unloved (b) guilty (c) sad (d) friendly (e) tired (f) angry (g) wistful (h) excited.

8. **Newly bereaved man:** "I've started to tidy up the garden this last week. She would have been pleased, you know. She was always nagging me about it and I never took much notice of her."

This man feels: (a) guilty (b) lost

(c) optimistic (d) at peace (e) distressed
(f) hostile (g) confident (h) regretful.

9. **Young soldier disabled by head injuries two years ago:** "I'll soon be back at work. I know it's up to me and I'll get these legs going again. It just takes time. Then I'll be back there with my mates. We'll soon be up to our tricks again".

This man feels: (a) realistic (b) defeated
(c) optimistic (d) desperate (e) adventurous
(f) frightened (g) unable to face reality (h) non-accepting of his situation (i) at peace.

10. **Adult stammerer:** "I don't see much point in being here. I've seen plenty of Speech Therapists before and none of them did anything for me. In fact, I've never been interested in doing anything about my speech. Why does it bother other people so much? It's a waste of everyone's time."

This person feels: (a) alarmed (b) angry
(c) resentful (d) fed up (e) at ease (f) bored
(g) competent (h) puzzled (i) cocky (j) awed.

EXERCISE C.
DECIDING WHAT TO SAY IN RESPONSE TO A PATIENT

The reader is invited to give some time to considering these short extracts, and then to formulate possible responses. Short summaries of how the therapist responded to these patients can be found in the Appendix. (page 69).

1. **Terminally ill patient:** "I know that I'm going to die, but I'm afraid that my husband doesn't realise it. He tends to depend on me a lot and I'm sure he's convinced I'll be back to normal within the next year."

What would you say? ———————————————

———————————————————————————————

———————————————————————————————

2. **Psychogenic voice patient:** "I really do want to get my voice back. I sound so silly like this. My husband says I've got a voice like a saw. He does say some things to me, you know. I wish I could get it back then he'd be happy again; but it just won't come."

What would you say? —————————————

——————————————————————————

——————————————————————————

3. **Psychogeriatric patient:** "I've been here for nearly a year now, you know. And they won't stop telling me these things. It comes in through my ears and it won't stop. All night it goes on and on."

What would you say? —————————————

——————————————————————————

——————————————————————————

4. **Patient following eight months' treatment:** "It's up to you, really, but I just don't think I'm getting any better. Can I stop coming to see you?"

What would you say? —————————————

——————————————————————————

——————————————————————————

5. **Wife of a geriatric patient who still remains in hospital:** "I wish I could have him home. He's desperate to get back to his own things and be with me. The nurses here are very good but it's not like your own home is it?

What would you say? —————————————

——————————————————————————

——————————————————————————

6. **Husband of patient who suffered a CVA three months ago:** "Yes, you've told me all that before, about you not being able to tell how long it will be before her speech comes back. But I'm not convinced with that. Is there a doctor I can see about this?"

What would you say—————————————————

—————————————————————————————————

—————————————————————————————————

7. **Mother of child with language delay:** "My sister was late talking and she didn't have speech therapy and she managed all right. I just don't see the point of all this fuss. Amy's all right, you know. She understands everything we say to her. I just don't think this is a good idea at all."

What would you say? ————————————————

—————————————————————————————————

—————————————————————————————————

8. **Patient with early symptoms of motor neurone disease:** "Well, so far I've been all right really. If it just stays like this then I'll have no problems. One of my wife's friends told her about someone who had died of motor-neurone disease. Is that right? I wish someone would explain more to me."

What would you say? ————————————————

—————————————————————————————————

—————————————————————————————————

9. **Patient:** "Of course, I have a really good marriage. My husband is most generous to me and the girls; and although he's away a lot, it doesn't seem to matter. We can lead our separate lives and get along quite well. He's been like that for years; since I had the miscarriage, actually.

What would you say? ————————————————

————————————————

————————————————

ROLE PLAY

Role play is the process of acting the part of a real or imagined person, a method often used in developing skills in counsellors. By applying this technique in training, participants can learn by experience just what it feels like to be 'the patient'. This is a most valuable way of gaining insight into the perceptions of a person in need of help; and it is generally more constructive than relying on abstract discussion of hypothetical cases.

By 'playing the role' of a patient known to you, or else by simulating a 'type' of patient, aspects of that person's perceptions can be explored. Frequently, issues will emerge to which one has previously given insufficient attention as the listener.

If possible, the reader is advised to find a colleague with whom to work on the following exercises. Ask the colleague to assume the role of therapist. Spend *at least* five minutes developing each role.

ROLE PLAY EXERCISES

(a) Imagine that you are a young mother. Your child has just been diagnosed as mentally handicapped. Tell your listener what you feel about this.

(b) Your husband is seriously ill in hospital. You are living on a farm 15 miles from the hospital and you have to take charge of running the farm, dealing as best you can with business matters, and looking after your four children who are all under 11 years old. Talk to your listener about how you feel.

(c) Your wife has been in and out of hospital for over a year. You do not feel that the doctors have told you exactly what is the matter with her; it is hard to get to talk to them; and anyway, you are rather nervous of doctors and the hospital atmosphere. However, you are extremely worried. Talk to your listener about how you feel.

Further points to consider

Having completed each of these exercises, try to think back over the sorts of things you said. Was there anything that would lead you to think in a different way about the person you attempted to role play?

The aim of these tasks is to highlight for the reader how important it is to have an open mind about people. It is inadvisable for a counsellor to have pre-conceived ideas, particularly when working with individuals whose background and/or life experiences are very different from one's own. Role play provides an opportunity to identify and modify unhelpful attitudes and to develop a wider range of potential responses.

Chapter 6
CLINICAL SITUATIONS

This chapter presents a series of cameos that highlight some of the ethical and emotional situations that therapists may encounter in the clinical setting. Readers are invited to consider what approach they would adopt in such circumstances, and then to read how the incident was handled in reality. It should be stressed that there is no one 'right' way to respond.

The following descriptions are intended to stimulate potential counsellors to examine critically these, and their own, responses to problems with which they may be confronted. A final section identifies some key issues for discussion.

1. **The mother of a young man** who had suffered encephalitis arrived unexpectedly in the clinic and asked to see the therapist. She said she felt she had to come and tell the therapist that the young man had lost interest in the exercises he had been set to do at home. Because of this, the patient's mother wanted to stop bringing her son for therapy as she felt it was wasting the therapist's time.

What would you do?
The therapist felt puzzled about why the mother had felt it necessary to do this. Certainly, she had not

noticed any particular lack of interest on the part of the patient. It was decided to encourage the mother to talk in more detail about why she had come to the clinic with this idea.

It transpired that the mother was under great strain herself; and transporting her son was proving an unwelcome extra burden. If the therapy appointments had been discontinued it would have meant one less thing to deal with. The therapist became actively involved in finding more support for the mother, and the frequency of clinic visits was temporarily reduced.

2. **The husband of a young woman** patient with a brain tumour broke down when talking to the therapist and confessed he was having an affair. He felt deeply distressed and guilty for, whilst being sure he could not leave his wife because of her illness, he also felt unable to maintain a close relationship with her because of his involvement with the other woman.

What would you do?
The potential for divided loyalties in this situation was very apparent to the professional. All those concerned were in an unenviable position; and there was no obvious solution to the dilemma, given the patient's distressing illness. It was judged appropriate not to extend the therapist's role with the husband to more than that of supportive listener, although he had apparently found it helpful to be able to talk about his feelings. The therapist continued to give regular help to the patient, this 'help' becoming purely supportive in time, as her condition deteriorated rapidly. Meanwhile, no attempt was made to intervene in the complicated family relationships. Within a year, the patient had died.

3. **The mother of a handicapped child** confided that her relationship with her husband was poor and getting worse all the time. The mother believed that this was attributable to the child's complicated needs and the husband's demanding job which involved a lot of travell-

ing. She confided that she often felt very neglected herself, because of the attention she had to give to her child. Whilst she wanted to tell her husband how difficult things were, she feared she would not find him sympathetic. She asked the therapist to talk to her husband, on the grounds that he would be more likely to take notice of the therapist.

What would you do?

The therapist felt most uncomfortable at the prospect of 'liaising' between husband and wife; and judged that this would be neither appropriate nor helpful. Furthermore, the fact that the wife believed so emphatically that she would not be able to 'get through' to her husband, led the therapist to believe that the wife's lack of confidence was actually a fundamental problem in the marriage. It seemed more important to focus the woman's attention on her lack of confidence, if this could be achieved.

There followed some exploration of how she perceived the way she related to her husband, and how she saw herself in her marriage. The discussion proved very helpful so a regular time was set aside for her to talk with the therapist on a weekly basis. After several months, the wife stated that she was feeling much better and had been able to face some of the difficulties with her husband. He had responded more readily than she had expected; and they were planning a short holiday together. Their child would be looked after by grandparents.

4. **A male patient with multiple sclerosis** had been hinting for some while about his unhappy marriage. Eventually, he broke down during a therapy session and described his loneliness in his marriage. Having been brought up to believe that it is not manly to show one's emotions, he clearly regretted this outburst, feeling he had lost face and was no longer the 'strong male' he wished to appear.

What would you do?

There were many problems in this session for the therapist. The patient had expressed some of his inner-most feelings and, by doing so, had revealed the degree of his respect for, and trust in, the therapist. Indeed, the therapist seemed to be the only person to whom he had ever dared express these feelings of vulnerability. At the same time, however, he appeared to have a deeply rooted concept of what 'being a man' entailed. The expression of intense emotion clashed unbearably with this notion and he felt he had 'lost face'.

Although attempts were made by the therapist to reassure him that being open and expressing one's feelings is normal and indeed helpful, the patient was not entirely convinced. He said he was ashamed at his outburst, and asked the therapist to forget what had taken place.

Two weeks later he asked to cancel his appointment; and, although the therapist wrote to him continuing to offer her support, the man declined to attend again.

The therapist had then to sort out her own feelings about this situation. There is always a fear that encouraging people to express strong emotions may give rise to an unmanageable intensity of feelings, resulting in some kind of damage. In this instance, it was understandable that the therapist should feel concerned. However, the most significant feature of that counselling session was the fact that the patient had, perhaps for the first time, been able to communicate some of his private, previously unacknowledged, emotions to another person. Although he believed at the time that he had done irrevocable damage to his image, there is a chance that, in the longer term, he may have obtained some benefit. On that particular occasion, the experience was perceived negatively, but the potential good effects might emerge when the man had absorbed this event as a part of his self concept.

The therapist concluded that the patient had in fact taken a positive step but had moved forward as far as he could at that time. He now needed to take stock of his situation.

5. **The mother of a nine-year-old boy** with a severe stammer at first appeared unwilling to talk about their home life. She eventually revealed that the boy's father, a man with a violent temper, sometimes hit the boy when he stammered. He was also violent with his wife; and she had once spent some time in a refuge for battered wives when the boy was small. However, she had found she could not manage without a man around, so had gone back to her husband.

This mother appeared to be of low average intelligence; and when questioned about the effect the father's violence had on her son, she said she sometimes thought it helped him 'pull himself together'.

What would you do?

The therapist judged that the major problem in this family would need further help, but that her primary commitment was to the child with the stammer; so she referred the family to a social worker. Meanwhile, the boy received an intensive course of therapy and was also given a lot of time for individual discussion with the therapist. It was felt that he was old enough to benefit from deeper discussion of his own feelings about his speech and his parents.

Although he did find it difficult to put into words how he felt, the therapist encouraged his communication by inviting him to do drawings of himself and his family. He produced several vivid pictures, including some which showed letters pouring out of his mouth in a long line. (These he described as his stammer coming out of his mouth.) The boy did talk about his father: sometimes he did not admit to minding about the violence in the home; but on other occasions, he spoke openly of fear of his father. The therapist reflected this ambivalence back to the boy, inviting him to think this through. In time, he was able to acknowledge the complexity of his feelings about his father, and the difficulties he experienced in wanting love from someone he also feared.

As the boy began to develop more control over his stammer, his self esteem increased. He also began to understand more fully the difficult situation at home, discussing with the therapist ways in which he might talk to his father and, incidentally, help his mother.

The therapist had been able to provide a supportive environment for him while he focused attention on improving his speech. During this period he was able to explore his own constructs more fully, and consider his relationship with his parents. Although very many problems persisted in that family environment, the boy had gained in confidence and was helped to re-evaluate the situation.

6. **A patient in her early twenties** who had suffered a stroke confided that she wanted to have a child when she and her fiancé married later that year. She had decided to go ahead and become pregnant without asking the advice of her doctor so that there would not be an opportunity for the doctor to advise against starting a family.

What would you do?

The therapist first wondered why the patient had confided in her, given that she was actually saying she wanted no medical intrusion. It was concluded that the young woman must really have some doubts about this plan and was first checking it out with her therapist, in the safety of their relationship. She was encouraged to talk about why she had decided to exclude the doctor. This led into a discussion of the patient's fears concerning her stroke and childbirth. The therapist was able to develop the dialogue by initial use of a closed question: was she worried in case the doctor might stop her from having a child? Although this was a disconcerting question to be asked outright, the patient appeared to be relieved to have her fears brought into focus. With the therapist, who she felt she could trust, she talked of the deep feelings she had about wanting a child, and how devastated she would be if a doctor advised against motherhood. The therapist said that she could well understand the woman's fears and the intensity of her feelings.

Whilst it was not possible to predict what the doctor might advise, reassurance was given that the patient's predicament would be taken seriously. The therapist continued to explore with the patient, her feelings about suffering a stroke and the distress she experienced at the time. It became clear that she had no wish to relive her stroke symptoms; and eventually, she came to accept that it would be wisest to explore the question of pregnancy with her doctor before taking any chances. This discussion and re-evaluation took place over a period of a few weeks. Subsequently, the young woman did see her doctor, and she was advised that it would be safe to start a family.

7. **A young man aged twenty two** who had been in a motor-cycle accident resulting in a moderate hemiplegia, announced to his married therapist one day that he had fallen in love with her. He said he wanted them to live together so he could be with her all the time, and that he could not stop thinking about her.

What would you do?
The therapist was alarmed by this, and found it difficult to decide how to respond constructively. The predicament was to find the right balance with this young man: if she dismissed this expression of his feelings as simply representing how lonely he was, there was a danger of sounding both patronising and rejecting. However, to respond to his statements in a totally accepting way would risk reinforcing the patient's mis-guided belief that there was some real potential for a closer personal relationship with his therapist.

She first acknowledged how the patient felt, saying that she understood his feelings were serious. It was then necessary to try to help the patient re-evaluate his feelings. He was encouraged to explore some of his thoughts about women in general, in the belief that this would give him a chance to develop a more realistic attitude to his therapist. It might be possible for him to recognise that the qualities which he found attractive in her — those of patience, warmth and concern — were qualities which can be found in very many women.

In this particular case, the therapist was able to maintain a supportive relationship with the young man over a period of months. During this time, his feelings for her became less intense as he analysed some of his ideas about women. He was also able to discuss with the therapist the re-emergence of his sexual drive which had been affected by the accident. He was distressed, understandably, at having no-one with whom to share his sexuality. Fortunately, during this period, he was introduced to a club for the physically disabled where he was able to talk about his feelings with other members. Here, he was able to form new relationships; and the patient was later successfully discharged.

8. **A psychogenic voice patient** told the therapist that her voice had 'started to go' around the time that her husband had his first heart attack, about three months ago. She commented that she had never lost her voice before and that she thought it must be due to the worry over her husband's health.

What would you do?

The therapist agreed that the voice problem must relate to the husband's illness, but was keen that the woman try to sort out some of her feelings about this. 'Worry', the therapist considered, was far too general a term. During a long discussion, it became apparent that this lady was dealing with a lot of anxiety about how she would manage alone, should her husband die. She reported that she often felt as if he were already dead, finding herself crying and mourning for him as if in advance of the event. Mixed with this anxiety was a great deal of anger with him for being ill and putting her in this insecure position. The patient, having developed great trust in the therapist, was able to express these feelings openly to her. She cried in their sessions together, and afterwards reported that she felt less overwhelmed. Immediately the patient began to express these feelings, her voice showed some signs of returning; and within three months, the voice was normal.

9. **A fourteen-year-old cerebral palsied girl** who was confined to a wheelchair, confided in her therapist about her dreams for the future. She believed that her faith in God would somehow work a cure for her and that when she was adult she would no longer be handicapped, but able to go dancing, meet a nice boy, marry and have children.

What would you do?
Startled by the apparent lack of realism, given the extent of the girl's handicaps, the therapist's first instinct was to attempt to help her face reality. However, it was decided to accept what the girl said in the session and otherwise to make no reference to it. Careful thought was later given to what had occurred, and the therapist judged it best not to bring the subject up again. The justification for this decision was that the girl, now in early adolescence, had a need for these dreams since they gave her something to believe in at that time in her life.

10. **A very withdrawn patient** told the therapist that he did not enjoy all the attention he was getting as a result of his hemiplegia. He said he had always been a very private person and that he did not appreciate everyone asking him questions about himself. In an outburst of intense emotion he said he felt he would be 'destroyed' by the therapist's continual curiosity.

What would you do?
The therapist was concerned about the strength of this man's feelings. The way that he had construed offers of help was clearly unusual, if not abnormal. To talk of being 'destroyed' by someone whose role was actually to take care of people, seemed to suggest that this patient

perhaps found any sort of personal closeness overwhelming and somehow threatening.

Up to this point, the therapist felt confident she had related to him in the same way that she had (apparently successfully) related to other patients. It was therefore decided to discuss this case with a clinical psychologist. She was advised that the patient's statements did suggest some sort of schizoid reaction, and that it would be wise not to pursue the issue at that time in case he responded by withdrawing further.

Regular discussions continued between psychologist and therapist. And only at a later stage in the patient's treatment, when he appeared to be more relaxed, did the therapist try to discover what he remembered of his feelings on that previous, emotional occasion. The patient found it extremely difficult to articulate anything about the event. He did, however, mention that he had received some psychiatric help six years before. When the therapist asked if he thought he would like to see a psychiatrist again, the man said he felt he was managing reasonably well now and did not want to have things 'stirred up' again. He said that sometimes he felt very overwhelmed, and that suffering a stroke had made him feel more vulnerable. It was decided to accept the patient's assessment of the situation which appeared reasonable. No further action was taken.

11. **A patient, recovering well from a road accident** which had occurred one year before, told her therapist on two separate occasions that she now felt very confused about her life. When asked directly what exactly was bothering her, she said she did not know, she was unable to work things out.

What would you do?
The therapist felt there were two possible approaches to this woman's problem. First, it might be sufficient simply to listen and then allow time to play a part, for feelings of confusion and loss of confidence are

natural in such circumstances. Alternatively, it might be more helpful to develop the patient's understanding of her situation by use of exploratory questions, and by reflecting back to her some of the points raised.

In this case, the latter approach was chosen. Instead of using open questions such as "How do you feel?" (which could only have produced a vague answer of "confused"), the therapist formulated questions which were more closed. (For example, "What is different about your life since the accident?") The concrete answers given to these questions led naturally into a clearer discussion about herself. The therapist also asked questions such as "Do you think you are a different person since your accident?"; "How?"; and "Do you think your family have changed in any way since your accident?" These provided a basis for helpful dialogue and a foundation upon which the young woman could reconstrue her situation.

12. **The stepmother of a child with severe language delay** confided that she found him extremely difficult to handle. This child was the youngest of three children; and the stepmother had married their father one year before. The woman was obviously very intelligent, had previously worked in a publishing firm, had no real experience of children, and had been an only child herself. Furthermore, she had moved to a different area when she married.

What would you do?

Before this lady approached the therapist for support, it had been observed that she was having some difficulties with the boy, and that these were causing distress. Since the stepmother herself identified the need for help, direct advice was given about handling him.

In view of the woman's evident frustration, it was also decided to explore indirectly with her, some of her feelings about taking on this ready-made family. The therapist had sensed that she was not fully committed to the idea of being a step-parent. Over a period of months, this woman used the time with the therapist to voice her distress at finding that she greatly missed the stimulating work she had been doing. She felt unsatisfied by her new role of looking after three children who were not hers. She frequently referred to herself as someone who "used to know how to cope, but now doesn't" and appeared to feel trapped in an alien existence.

Over the period reported, the stepmother became more relaxed with the little boy. She also found the courage to discuss some of her feelings openly with her husband. He had not appreciated that she was finding the situation so difficult, and subsequently became much more supportive.

DISCUSSION POINTS

1. Patients or relatives may volunteer information which they will expect to be withheld from all other people, because of confidentiality. Are there any situations in which the breaking of confidentiality can be justified?

2. Although the aim of this type of counselling is to be non-directive, are there any situations where it might be appropriate to speak from one's own experience and offer direct advice?

3. In what instances is it perhaps better to allow patients to cherish pipedreams? Should one try to steer them, through counselling, towards greater realism?

4. Therapists may see many patients with progressive conditions. If they confide that they would prefer to die now, before becoming totally disabled, what would be the appropriate response? What are the reader's thoughts on this very sensitive issue?

5. In what circumstances might it appear more appropriate to take no action instead of providing counselling?

It may prove impossible to arrive at any firm conclusions about the above issues, but time spent in considering these and other difficult clinical decisions will not have been wasted.

CONCLUSION

Using counselling skills in clinical work can be a rewarding and exciting experience. The patient who finds he can talk about his feelings demonstrates that he values and trusts his therapist, and feels secure in their relationship.

Counselling involves a two-way process. The patient or client shares his deepest feelings with the counsellor, in response to the security and warmth which you extend to him. It must be emphasised to all would-be and developing counsellors that, as part of the two-way process, a patient's feelings frequently have a profound impact on the listener: intense distress may cause you sadness; anger may frighten you; despair may wear you down. Counsellors must learn to examine their own reactions to patients, for the way they respond will undoubtedly influence the future outcome of any interaction. If frightened or overwhelmed, the therapist would be strongly advised to talk to a colleague about it. One's own reactions cannot be discounted from the equation, and it is most important to learn to be honest with oneself.

As stated at the beginning of this book, no script can be provided for the counsellor: assisted by the approaches presented in this book, the therapist must feel his or her own way. If it is possible to use a colleague (from either the same or a different profession) as an informal supervisor with whom cases can be discussed, this can prove extremely valuable. In time, one develops greater confidence in one's own reactions. However, there will always be a proportion of more difficult cases about which such discussion would be helpful.

If a patient seems to be making negligible progress, appearing to be going over the same ground again and again, he should not be dismissed or abandoned. People who are coming to terms with emotional issues often take longer than one might predict. The therapist should remain patient and sensitive, however slowly changes may occur, for it is not possible to modify deep-rooted constructs in a hurry. Speck (1978), in summarising the help that can be offered to people who are grieving, makes this simple statement:

> *"Whatever else we may be able to offer to those in need, one very important gift is that of time".*

APPENDIX I

Exercise A (page 35)

ORDER OF OPENNESS OF QUESTIONS

Most open

1. How are you?
2. What sort of things does she say to you?
3. How do you get on talking to strangers?
4. Shall I fetch you something from the shop?
5. When did you have your stroke?
6. At what age did she sit up?
7. Would you like cream with these strawberries?

Least open

Exercise B (page 44)

INTERPRETING HOW THE PATIENT FEELS

1. *Woman recovering from road accident:* peaceful; positive; surprised; grateful; relieved

2. *Parent of mentally handicapped adult:* distressed; realistic; preoccupied

3. *Geriatric patient:* distressed; empty; grief-stricken; hopeless

4. *Transexual male who wants to change to a female:* unrealistic; optimistic; self confident; idealistic

5. *Wife of man who suffered a CVA three months ago:* bewildered; lost; tired

6. *Adult physically handicapped man:* angry; misunderstood; indignant; isolated

7. *Child with specific learning difficulties:* guilty; sad; tired; wistful

8. *Newly bereaved man:* guilty; lost; distressed; regretful

9. *Young soldier disabled by head injury two years ago:* frightened; unable to face reality; non-accepting of his situation

10. *Adult stammerer:* angry; resentful; fed up; puzzled

Exercise C (page 47)

DECIDING WHAT TO SAY IN RESPONSE TO A PATIENT

As previously mentioned, there can be no set script in counselling. What we can do, however, is to consider what *sort* of response is most appropriate to what a patient has said.

The following short extracts summarise how the therapist approached these real situations, but it must be emphasised that they can only serve as suggestions or points for discussion.

1. *Terminally ill patient:*

Therapist: *"Then that must make you feel very cut off from him at the moment. What do you feel about taking the initiative yourself and starting to ask your husband what he feels like at the moment?"*

2. *Psychogenic voice patient:*

Therapist: *"It sounds as if it's very important to please your husband. Does your voice problem upset him a lot?"* (*In this case, much exploration ensues to find out about her husband's reaction to her voice and her own feelings about her voice loss, her marriage, etc.*)

3. *Psychogeriatric patient:*

Therapist: *"That must be very uncomfortable for you. Can you tell me what sort of things they are saying?"*

4. *Patient following eight months' treatment:*
Therapist: *"Can you tell me what's made you feel like that today? Why do you think you aren't getting any better?*

5. *Wife of a geriatric patient who still remains in hospital:*
Therapist: *"I know; hospital is not the same. When is the last time you talked to Sister? Perhaps she could give you some idea of how much longer it will be."*

6. *Husband of patient who suffered a CVA three months ago:*
Therapist: *"Yes, there are several doctors who you can talk to if you want. But can you try to tell me what makes you feel like this?"*

7. *Mother of child with language delay:*
Therapist: *"I know you don't like the idea of it at all and I am quite concerned about you feeling this way. I certainly feel very concerned and worried about Amy. Children vary a lot in the difficulties they have, and I think we need to sort out whether your sister's and Amy's difficulties are similar. Can you tell me more about what sort of difficulty your sister had and how it cleared up?"*

8. *Patient with early symptoms of motor neurone disease:*
Therapist: *"Of course, you really do need to have a long talk with one of the doctors. Who did you see in the clinic? What did he say to you then?"*

9. *Patient:*
Therapist: *"Why doesn't it seem to matter?" (Further exploration is needed here to find out more about how the patient perceived her marriage to be good.)*

COMMENT

Note that all of these responses firstly acknowledge the theme of what the patient has been saying. It is then appropriate to take the conversation further by exploring some aspect of what was said: something that needs further clarification. This is done by using a question at the end of the response.

Bibliography

Bannister, D & Fransella, F, *Inquiring Man*, 2nd ed, Penguin, 1980

Bowlby, J, *Loss, Sadness and Depression: Attachment and Loss*, vol 3, Penguin, 1981

Broida, H, *Coping with Stroke: Communication Breakdown with Brain-injured Adults,* College Hill Press, 1979.

Brumfitt, S M, 'Time to raise a voice', *The Remedial Therapist* (3), no 22, 1981, p6

Brumfitt, S M, 'Another side to therapy', *The Bulletin of the College of Speech Therapists*, May 1985, no 397

Brumfitt, S M, 'The use of repertory grids with aphasic people', in *Repertory Grid Technique and Personal Constructs – applications in clinical and educational settings*, (ed) N Beail, Croom Helm, London, 1985

Brumfitt, S M and Clarke, P R F, 'An application of psychotherapeutic techniques to the management of aphasia', in C Code and D Muller, *Aphasia Therapy*, Edward Arnold, 1983

Clarke, P R F, 'The "medical model" defended', *New Society*, January 9, 1975

Corney, M, 'A lost child lives on', *New Forum: The Journal of the Psychology and Psychotherapy Association*, March 1981

Dahlberg, C C and Jaffe, J, *Stroke: a Doctor's Diary of his Recovery*, G McLeod Ltd, US & Canada, 1977

Darvill, G, 'Rehabilitation – not just voice', in *Laryngectomy – Diagnosis to Rehabilitation*, (ed) Y Edels, Croom Helm, 1983

Dembo, T, Ladieu-Leuiton, G. Wright, B A, 'Acceptance of loss – amputation' in *Psychological Aspects of Physical Disabilities*, (ed) J Garret, Washington, DC, US Government Printing Office, 1952

Ellis, A, *Reason and Emotion in Psychotherapy*, Lyle Stuart, New York, 1962

Freud, S, *Mourning and Melancholia* (in *The Complete Psychological Works of Sigmund Freud*, vol 14, Hogarth Press, London, 1958)

Goffman, E, *Stigma*, Penguin, 1963

Guntrip, H, *Personality Structure and Human Interaction*, Hogarth Press, 1961

Hinton, J, *Dying*, Penguin, 1967

Horney, K, *Neurosis and Human Growth,* New York, 1950

James, W, *The Principles of Psychology*, Macmillan & Co, 1890

Kelly, G, *The Psychology of Person Constructs*, vols 1 & 2, Norton & Co, New York, 1955

Kessler, H, 'Psychological preparation of the amputee', *Industrial Medicines*, 10:107, 1951

Kovel, J, *A Complete Guide to Therapy,* Pelican, 1976

Kubler-Ross, E, *Death – the Final Stage of Growth*, Prentice-Hall, Englewood Cliffs, 1975

Laing, R, *The Divided Self*, Pelican, 1969

Laing, R D, *The Self and Others*, Pelican, 1969

Lewis, C S, *A Grief Observed*, Faber & Faber, 1966

Luria, A R, *The Man with a Shattered World*, Penguin, 1972

Maguire, P and Hampson, M, 'The operation was successful but the patient wants to die . . .', *World Medicine*, November 3, 1976, p 35-7

Mead, G, *Mind, Self and Society*, University of Chicago Press, 1934

Moustakas, C (ed), *The Self-explorations in Personal Growth*, Harper & Row, 1956

Parkes, C M, *Bereavement*, Pelican, 1975

Parkes, C M, 'Psychological transitions – comparisons between reactions to loss of a limb and loss of a spouse', *British Journal of Psychiatry*, 127, 1975, p 204-210

Patterson, C H, *Theories of Counselling and Psychotherapy*, Harper & Row, 1973

Perls, F, *Gestalt Therapy Verbatim*, Bantam, 1972

Rogers, C, *Client Centred Therapy*, Houghton Mifflin, Boston, 1951

Rogers, C, *On Becoming a Person*, Constable, 1961

Rowan, J, *Ordinary Ecstasy*, Routledge & Kegan Paul, 1976

Rowe, D, *The Experience of Depression*, John Wiley & Sons, 1978

Safilios-Rothschild, C, *The Sociology and Social Psychology of Disability and Rehabilitation*, Random House, New York, 1970

Shibutani Tomatsu, *Society and Personality*, Englewood Cliffs, N J, Prentice Hall, 1961

Skinner, B F, *Science and Human Behaviour*, Collier Macmillan, 1953

Strauss, A, 'Transformation of Identity' (in *Human Behaviour and Social Processes*, (ed) A M Rose, Houghton Mifflin, Boston, 1962)

Skenderian, D, 'Psychological aftermath of stroke: reflections of a personal construct psychologist' paper presented at Fifth International Conference on Personal Construct Psychology, Boston, Massachusetts, 1983

Speck, P, *Loss and Grief in Medicine*, Bailliere Tindall, 1978

Wolpe, J, *The Practice of Behaviour Therapy*, Oxford, 1969

Wolpe, J, *Psychotherapy by Reciprocal Inhibition*, Stanford University Press, 1958

Wright, B A, *Physical Disability – a psychological approach*, 2nd ed, Harper & Row, 1983